Know My Voice I

THE MYSTERY OF THE THREAD OF ISRAEL

by

Rev. Dr. John Diomede

To order additional copies of this book, contact:
Proisle Publishing Services LLC
1177 6th Ave 5th Floor
New York, NY 10036, USA
Phone: (+1 347-922-3779)
info@proislepublishing.com

My Sheep Know My Voice

My sheep listen to my voice; I know them, and they follow me. [28] I give them eternal life, and they shall never perish; no one will snatch them out of my hand. (Joh 10:27-28 NIV)

Dedicated to:

Parker

Scarlett

Addy

Table of Contents

Introduction

It is imperative for us to do the best we can do and be the best we can be in our efforts at relationships. This includes with family, while raising children, while in the workplace, with friends and even with those we do not know. We achieve this principle by being cognizant of life, our participation thereof, and our efforts to overcome the voices that distract us from acting with love, compassion, and mercy. As we observe ourselves on this journey, we must also have a sense of integrity and consistency in this process. Adherence to this process informs us of who we are at our core. We have many occurrences in life that distract us from being the best that we can be while on this road. And, if you are like me, the challenges are numerous, serious, and consistent. Nowhere is this effort more important than our awareness of God, than our relationship with God, and our familiarity with the voice of God, the Holy Spirit. I encourage you to make the effort in considering the significance and value of not letting religion get in the way of this relationship. It is vitally important.

The Soap Box

Is God a mystery? Does God communicate with humanity? Is communication restricted to audible hearing, the bible, religious organizations? Are people a mystery? What do we really know about living beings? I have a profound interest in both God and humanity and the interaction thereof. I am interested in what I can learn about the human to human and the human-to-God relationship. What makes us tick, have ideas, interests, passions? Why do we like? Why do we dislike? From where do our thoughts, thought processes, decisions, and conclusions emanate? Why do I think about what I think about? Over time I have come to realize that I learn the answers to these questions about myself and others primarily through observing the soapbox. You know that imaginary platform for me, or someone else, from which to publicly air views and opinions. Sometimes it is difficult to find because some individuals are not substantially motivated to put forth their views for some reason or another, but it exists within each of us. Given the proper moment or set of circumstances, it will surface. My soapbox is considering the active relationship between the God of the bible and the human being, and in some manner disseminate that information to others. As I move along on my journey here, serious consideration of the departure from this realm seems all too insignificant to humanity until and if that time comes into view. Without being morbid, it seems wise to attain the best understanding we can on the topic. The bible and the God presented in its pages, as I will explain, is the source, means, and climax of this matter. That being said, knowing His voice, the voice of the Holy Spirit is the best advantage one can have to solidify their life and comprehend the journey.

Lanes of Preconception

As we approach this exercise, the challenge to consider is the idea of preconception. Years ago, I began to discover that I had attitudes or lanes of thinking when it came to God and people. Over time, the various lanes that existed in my thoughts and actions became more and more evident. One of the first exercises I encourage you to consider is to recognize your lanes and expose them to some scrutiny. Unfortunately, my process took some time so, it will not be easy in this short writing for you to engage in an extended look at yourself. My hope is that with help of the Holy Spirit, you can move the process along daily in order to learn more about yourself and God.

I was brought up in religion and considered it important to be religious. It was a way of life, an important way of life. The religious experience ran deep for various reasons. That depth was never harsh or severe, it simply was a way of life. But it was an exacting way. You can imagine my surprise when I experienced a very unexpected development. I began to scrutinize my lanes of thinking. I needed to begin to identify and challenge many preconceived ideas I had about God, religion, faith, organizations, the concept of words such as holy, sin, judgement, punishment, the concept of good, evil, right, wrong and more. After I became a licensed minster, I began to recognize that the manner in which I understood these words and concepts formed the lanes of my thoughts and conclusions. It is not that these words do not have meaning, it is that their meanings, in many ways, have been skewed and boxed in throughout the existence of humanity. When it comes to the relationship between God and human, the greatest injustice we do to the experience is to box it in from the outset because of what we think we know. For example, if I say the word democrat, republican, Jew, Hindu, Baptist, or Catholic, immediately the human mind begins to process its knowledge, bias, understanding, and conclusions about that word. In other words, the word is more than a word, it is a complex idea that is already established and concluded in our mind. So, what is my goal about this God relationship? Did you ever have a conclusion on a past matter in your life that became suspect whereby you had to change that conclusion? This is exactly that to which I am referring. Here is a little bit of my process on the topic.

God's Dwelling

God has brought me in and out of several movements of church organizations, theological and philosophical thought, and human relational understanding. Where religion is concerned, I was born into Roman Catholicism, broke out of that organizational mindset into the movement known as Pentecostalism, escaped that identification into the sect known as Messianic Judaism, and finally broke free to understand the relational experience of hearing from the Holy Spirit of God directly, free from organizational and religious preconception. This process did take the Holy Spirit some years to untrain and liberate me from a religious approach and convince me how exactly God dwells in a person. The most interesting part being that the biblical text was right there in front of me. It simply took hearing it from God's perspective to begin the journey.[1] Keep in mind, it is not my goal to disparage the organizations or movements mentioned. I simply realize that they contained distractions that were not beneficial to this final lifestyle. Distractions that are not visible to the religious. Take into consideration the following. The focus of every one of those movements, or organizations that those movements produced, are mostly hidden,

---

[1] 13 But when he, the Spirit of truth, comes, he will guide you into all the truth. He will not speak on his own; he will speak only what he hears, and he will tell you what is yet to come. 14 He will glorify me because it is from me that he will receive what he will make known to you. (Joh 16:13-14 NIV)

and at times obviously contrary to the purpose of this writing, which is about hearing from God without the organization. A clearly biblical teaching of Jesus himself. Also consider that while the organizations that I mentioned are Christian in nature, they are no different than any religious organization that exists on the face of the earth, they all eliminate the direct relationship with The Holy Spirit, and literally, the moment-by-moment interaction[2] with God. Why do I believe my point of view is accurate? Because the Holy Spirit cannot interact with an organization, The Holy Spirit interacts with human beings, individual human beings like you and me. Organizations with religious doctrines and dogma are substantively opposed to this, even if they say they are not. That is why they need doctrines, build edifices and collect offerings.[3] Their leaders must perpetuate the organization, the structure, the titles, and the deception. Sometimes with intent and other times ignorantly. God's purpose and plan where humanity and His Holy Spirit are concerned

---

[2] [28] So Jesus said, "When you have lifted up the Son of Man, then you will know that I am he and that I do nothing on my own but speak just what the Father has taught me. (Joh 8:28 NIV)

[3] [13] "Woe to you, teachers of the law...... you hypocrites! You shut the door of the kingdom of heaven in people's faces. You yourselves do not enter, nor will you let those enter who are trying to. (Mat 23:13 NIV)

is contained in the bible, but it is not restricted to the bible. It is an ongoing dynamic relationship that each human can partake of daily if they choose. I hope to make more visible this personal relationship for you.

Israel, Gentiles, and the Thread

Israel is the cultural group that God chose biblically with one primary purpose. The purpose was to be able to trace a physical line through which to bring the Messiah. Some think the plan is great and some think the plan is not so great. Both camps' arguments hinge singularly on Jesus being the Messiah, a major rift in religious thought and teaching.[4] That said, religious lanes of thinking cause the colossal misinterpretation of God, His plan, His Messiah, and His people. God wanted relationship with people. Prior to Moses, we see in the Bible that individuals had relationship with God, heard from God, worked for God, walked with God, and, up until Moses, we never really saw a full culturally

---

[4] Jesus answered, "I am the way and the truth and the life. No one comes to the Father except through me. (Joh 14:6 NIV)

organizational example of this relationship. But after God brought Israel out of bondage in Egypt, the relationship still was not with the organization, it was with an intermediary, namely Moses. How were all these biblical individuals, even post Moses, connected to God? There was a line, a connection, a historical "thread" that you could follow, such that if you yanked it, one could see exactly who was connected. The biblical list of individuals is not comprehensive, it is simply a pattern. As mentioned, the cultural aspect fulfilled the need for a traceable physical human line for the Messiah. It is the individual aspects that are of huge importance. One of the people on the thread was Jacob, later renamed Israel. Israel, the person, was committed to God eventually. While he was also a broken human, he clung to this relationship with the God of his father Abraham. We have the biblical account of Israel (Jacob) that only reveals a part of this relationship. I believe that the most significant part of his life spent with God was what is not recorded. It must be because it was the majority of his life! Their relationship is only highlighted by the biblical narrative. The result became a cultural group that contained people and promises from God that would affect the entire gentile world. Thru Israel (the descendants of Jacob connected to the thread) God kept the plan alive. So, God directed Moses to lead this cultural manifestation. The problem is that while the spiritual aspect lends itself to Israel functioning as the chosen people, the human aspect led Israel, as a nation, to become like every other nation. That is, a religious organization that operated religiously by binding itself to a format, not the Being of God. They mimicked other nations instead of being people that other nations could learn from. Religiously speaking, no other god manifested itself to humanity as did the God of Israel so while Israel as an organization failed, individuals of Israel maintained the connection to this thread, the witness of God, and produced the King of the Jews, Jesus of Nazareth. This uniqueness indicates God's desire to have relationship with humans and maintenance of His connection to the descendants of Israel and to ingrafted gentiles who make up this group of individuals attached to the thread. These statements continue to be true about God's relationship to individuals and to His disconnect to religious organizations right up to present day.[5] Lastly, one of

---

[5] He has shown you, O mortal, what is good. And what does the LORD require of you? To act justly and to love mercy and to walk humbly with your God. (Mic 6:8 NIV)

the proofs of this conclusion is found in the letters to the churches in the book of Revelation. The letters are to the organizations, because of mankind's attachment to earthly organizations. But the penalties and rewards are to the individuals. The relationship with God is bound to the individual.

Born Of God

To dig a little deeper into this point, the apostle Paul, a Jew, who concluded that Jesus was the Jewish Messiah and decided to follow Jesus as the Messiah, records some interesting passages in his writings. One of particular importance is found in the book of Romans. He states:

> *6 It is not as though God's word had failed. For not all who are descended from Israel are Israel. 7 Nor because they are his descendants are, they all Abraham's children. On the contrary, "It is through Isaac that your offspring will be*

> *reckoned." [8] In other words, it is not the children by physical descent who are God's children, but it is the children of the promise who are regarded as Abraham's offspring. Rom 9:6 NIV*

What does Paul mean when he says this? In some ways we think of bloodline in a manner that supersedes all other characteristics, relationally speaking. But in God's case, the thread that connects citizens of His Kingdom was not and is not blood[6]. If one were to adopt a child and raise that child as their own, while that child was not part of their bloodline, that child could in fact become more a part of the family culture than someone with a biological connection. Take for example when Israel was marching against Jericho, and they sent spies into the city. Rahab, a prostitute, harbored and helped those men. She was ultimately saved from the destruction of Jericho because she was connected to the thread, she was "of Israel" or "Abraham's offspring", which, in her case, had nothing to do with blood, it was

---

[6] But as many as received Him, to them He gave the right to become children of God, *even* to those who believe in His name, [13] who were born not of blood, nor of the will of the flesh, nor of the will of man, but of God. (Joh 1:12-13 NAS)

related to her inner decision-making process. She was a gentile born of God. What connected her to this thread? Rahab is also mentioned in the Bible as actually being a direct part of the ancestry of Jesus the Messiah.[7] This is true about two other women in the bible, Ruth, and Tamar, who also were not of the Israelite bloodline. It is clear that the bloodline of true Israel has less to do with blood and more to do with some other characteristic. The characteristics are found in the bible and exist in the hearts of God's people, people who accept the Jewish Messiah Jesus and people within whom the Holy Spirit dwells. God will bring about His plan for Abraham's offspring, the Israel made up of Jew and Gentile. He will bring about his plans for the Jews, Jacob's blood line on the thread. Additionally, Jesus, the King of the Jews will reign on his throne in Jerusalem. Comprehensive study of all these truths is not the focus of this writing so we will continue with the "thread".

---

[7] Salmon the father of Boaz, whose mother was Rahab, Boaz the father of Obed, whose mother was Ruth, (Mat 1:5 NIV)

The Religious Experience

How did we arrive where we are today when it comes to religious organizations? One remarkably interesting fact is that it appears, humanly speaking, the longer the roots of the group or organization, the more valid their existence. This is a major fallacy. Organizationally speaking, since bloodline is not relevant in most religions, to produce the religious experience, religion and religious organizations tend to think that their process or liturgy is something that is relevant, in other words, it will bring people closer to God. Or it may be that it will remind people of God. Or it may make people feel like they are obeying God. They may even feel holy. These all can be true while not coming within a hundred miles of an actual growing relationship with God.[8] [9] It is God that brings people closer to Himself. Jesus said he will be with us always even to the end. He manages that relationship through the Holy Spirit, whom He sent to us so that we may have relationship with Him and the

---

[8] Jesus said to her, "Woman, believe Me, an hour is coming when neither in this mountain, nor in Jerusalem, shall you worship the Father. (Joh 4:21 NAS)

[9] But an hour is coming, and now is, when those truly submitted shall worship the Father in spirit and truth; for such people the Father seeks to be His worshipers. God is spirit, and those who worship Him must worship in spirit and truth. (John 4:22–24 MW)

Father. It is the Holy Spirit who is the Standard of God's Israel. This is a group composed of both Jews and many gentile people groups based on individual connection to God thru the Holy Spirit. It is the Holy Spirit who is relevant. It is the Holy Spirit that does the work. It is the Holy Spirit that is the thread.

The Bible vs Religion

Like me, religious organizations all employ the Bible in some way to attain their goal. Some of them challenge their adherents to read the Bible or to "get into" the Bible more than others. Unfortunately, that practice does not necessarily produce any more of a relationship with the Holy Spirit than the ones who do not. Many religious organizations use habits, such as corporate prayers, weekly meetings, specific holy day celebrations and more. What is the purpose of these practices? Let us consider some of these behaviors or traditions. As mentioned earlier, I was born and raised Roman Catholic, and have in my walk with the Lord managed to remain in what can be referred to as Christianity to present day. I was raised with a cultural experience of Christmas, all saint's day, the immaculate conception, Easter, and more. Later in my Messianic Judaism experience, I became familiar with and celebrated Passover, Sukkot, Yom Kippur, and Rosha Shana. While I currently still celebrate some of these because of the cultural familial connections, my religious connection to them has faded. It has faded because I learned that you can do something out of habit and never manage to connect those habits to the God responsible for them, for example, taking communion. Many times, communion, in many denominations, is taken but the individual fails at the greater truth, I know I did.[10] Because of this truth, I do not necessarily refer to myself as a Christian anymore because Christianity, like all religions, does not embody basic biblical concepts such as being broken in spirit. My choice of description would be a "citizen of the Kingdom of God", which I mention because I use the term in this and other writings of mine.

---

[10] The sacrifices of God are a broken spirit; A broken and a contrite heart, O God, Thou wilt not despise. (Psa 51:17 NAS)

Jesus, The Center of The Universe

To better understand the fallacy my writing attempts to expose, there are two useful expressions in my repertoire. They are "organization centric" and "God centric". Simply put, one makes God central, the other places the organization central. There is nothing wrong with celebrating holidays and developing habits unless they become organizational centric. The original purpose of Thanksgiving was God centric but has today become organization centric, the organization of the United States. It is a cultural tradition that, in some cases, does not even begin the meal thanking God for His provision. There is nothing wrong with going to a religious worship service or some other weekly, monthly, or yearly organizational gathering unless they become organization centric. I myself participate in both culturally relevant and religiously relevant occasions because not to participate would be more of a distraction to others. But for me, they possess little relational substance with my God. One's relationship with God must be central. It must be grounded in relationship with the Holy Spirit. And because Jesus sent the Holy Spirit, it must be centered in his command to maintain relationships with others and to demonstrate that God wants a relationship with each individual human beyond the organizational experience.[11] This is the message of Jesus, and this is why he is the center of the universe

Who Is The Message For?

How do we replace organization relationship with God-relationship? When we say a prayer, such as the Our Father or The Shema, is it for the participant or the observer? When we wear a religious article like a cross or the Star of David or a prayer shawl, is it for the wearer or the observer? <u>If it's for the wearer or the participant, then the purpose must be to remind that individual of the connection they can have with God.</u> Israel was supposed to be a kingdom of priests. God intended they be a witness to the nations. Does being a witness to the nations involve being observed for the purpose of the

---

[11] But Moses replied, "Are you jealous for my sake? I wish that all the LORD's people were prophets and that the LORD would put his Spirit on them!" (Num 11:29 NIV)

observer or does it mean to "participate" for the purpose of the participant? One might say that it involves both. But is there a "primary" purpose, an order? Can one build a second story of a building without the first?[i] I believe the primary goal is to change the participant, or the doer, on the inside so they are constantly reminded to interact with the Holy Spirit. Therefore, Citizens of the Kingdom, at some point, understand God's plan, enact change, and as a result demonstrate a witness to others. The result occurs after the change. Consider Noah. He was heartbroken over the state of humanity, so he acted in God's direction! The bible says he was constantly tormented by human behavior. This was because he saw the world thru God's eyes. God's message was for Noah so he could complete the task at hand. The Kingdom citizen progresses inside out. Yes, others saw the message but, in this case their hearts were not turned. What is the message God is giving you?

Seeing What God Sees

The citizen of the Kingdom that has the thread of the Holy Spirit running through them somehow views life through God's principles, not doctrine or dogma. Gods' ways not human ways. That is why we cannot seem to put a finger on God, why the bible seemingly at times is contradictory or why organizations need additional doctrine to define "exactly" what God was intending when we see Him act in biblical events. Kingdom Citizens, somehow, are sensitive to the dynamic relationship that connects them directly to God. This relationship is with God's Spirit. The voice of God on the inside causing decisions to be made from the viewpoint of another, the viewpoint of the Holy Spirit. This is the viewpoint that considers how someone else see's a situation.[12] Jesus saw the need for compassion, that is exactly what he delivered to us. People tend to develop different perspectives after having children. They must become a parent. A doctor may develop a different perspective if they contract the same disease that they treat in others. When this relational perspective occurs with the Holy Spirit, that individual demonstrates a desire to see God's will be done and to participate in that process. Religion sees it different. It gets a bit thought-

---

[12] *Jesus straightened up and asked her, "Woman, where are they? Has no one condemned you?"* [11] *"No one, sir," she said. "Then neither do I condemn you," Jesus declared. "Go now and leave your life of sin.* (Joh 8:10-11 NIV)

provoking when we begin to combine our knowledge or understanding of religion with some of the biblical examples. The organizational idea of religion, especially where Christianity is concerned, is a goal of perfection through actions. This is not the biblical principle. No one, except Jesus, was perfect. Jesus sympathized with our brokenness because this is The Father's perspective. Moses disobeyed God. David disobeyed God. Others disobey God. I have disobeyed God. When a person lives out a portion of their faith by habit, say attending church regularly or any of the multitude of religious habits that exist, and then breaks that faith in some way (sinning), God's perspective is compassion. But, is a sinner the kind of witness that God is looking for in his people? Unfortunately, there is not any other kind of witness, we are all broken in some way! As a teacher, one of the points that always comes back to revisit me is that what I teach I must live, otherwise, observers of my life will observe me as a hypocrite and thus God becomes null and void. This, my friends, is the heart of the problem. My teachings come from having an ongoing relationship with God inside, which connects me to the thread. If I fail outwardly, I simply make it evident that I am like all the other citizens of the Kingdom, broken! Does this change God, or does it simply change one's opinion of God? The Kingdom Citizen then approaches the throne of grace in humility and asks for forgiveness. The prayer the Our Father is a good example, it is an individual prayer. Again, the thread is that God reaches into each individual human experience exclusively to bring about His Kingdom in the person. My teaching versus my habits may not necessarily be the relevant issue. What is relevant is that I have relationship with God and that I desire this relationship and that together with the Holy Spirit I fix the brokenness of my life a segment at a time, knowing that I will never really be able to correct it all. Any human can be connected to the thread of Israel, which is The Holy Spirit, in fact it is the Spirits desire to have this connection. Performance is for actors. Being is for the Kingdom citizens. Being a true Israelite, a child of Abraham, has to do with interaction using one's faith muscle and believing it in thought word, and deed and being consistent with that relationship. And here is a big AND, like Moses or David or any human, I am not perfect in the *doing* aspect. It is the hearing and being aspect that matters. It is this voice, The Voice of the Holy Spirit, encouraging me every day of who I am, His child, a citizen of His Kingdom and to continue to make His voice and guidance relevant in me so I may live for God in as many of my daily interactions as possible.

A Work in Progress

The witness of the Kingdom's citizen is supposed to start inside the individual and work its way outside. This means each human is a work in progress. The mystery of Israel was that they were supposed to be a separate people and the work should occur within each of them. Take the idea of circumcision. Circumcision is a reminder for the individual because it is on a part of the body that the individual does not display publicly. Only the individual see's the reminder. God's laws are supposed to be cemented in, written on the heart of the individual and work their way out of the individual by the participation of the individual moment by moment as the Spirit leads. And just like circumcision, the Holy Spirit's relationship is to be a reminder to the individual of who they are to God. Therefore, Jesus said, "I'm sending the Holy Spirit and He will guide you."[13] The Holy Spirit will guide each of us inside, so we can then turn those principles like mercy, compassion, and acting justly, outward. The outward part of Israel was that other nations would know that they had a different God and that their God was committed to them! And maybe, because of this relationship, people from the other nations would find the God of Israel thru the same relationship.

The Organization of the Messiah

Why is it that the organizations that seem to represent the church failed at their mission? They have failed for exactly the reasons I mentioned above. These churches, like other religious organizations, believe that what they are doing is for the observers. That their actions should demonstrate to others that this is where God wants you to be and how He wants you to act. However, at the same time, the leadership is responsible

---

[13] But when he, the Spirit of truth, comes, he will guide you into all the truth. He will not speak on his own; he will speak only what he hears, and he will tell you what is yet to come. (Joh 16:13 NIV)

for the people failing at the individual relationship with God because the adherent's relationship is really with the organization and its leaders. Many of my peers may disagree on this point with their words, but their actions say the contrary. They are always quick to make sure you know exactly where to send the offering check! Yet, they fail to realize that the Holy Spirit is for people's growth, benefit, and accountability. And by the way, the Holy Spirit is given freely. Jesus paid the price already. Now, you may also say to me, "But look at how long the church has been around -- it has lasted throughout the centuries." Yes, the organizations have lasted, one following the next. Citizens of the Kingdom broke free at various stages, only to have the next organization form and fail. And so, the process is repeated even up to today. What has really existed throughout the centuries is the organization of Jesus the Messiah. This is the Holy Spirit offering hope to a people who want a city built by God. The Holy Spirit working on people to drive them toward God[14] and away from their human brokenness. Church organizations have come and gone.

---

[14] All these people were still living by faith when they died. They did not receive the things promised; they only saw them and welcomed them from a distance, admitting that they were foreigners and strangers on earth. (Heb 11:13 NIV)

The largest ones having incorporated so much cultic behavior into their liturgy's that they more represent the enemies of God than God. We have glimpses back thru the Biblical culture of Israel. Organizations use these glimpses of biblical culture in an attempt to duplicate the religion we read about in the bible. Because of this, we have seen organizational success littered with individual failure, hurt, and brokenness. What we need to duplicate are the inward manifestations that the biblical examples gave us, the relationship with the Spirit of God.

Echad

I have become very focused about the word *Echad*.[15] *Echad* is how God describes His being. *Echad* means unity, unit, one. God has been talking to me about *Echad* and asking me why I display it on my person, my hat, and on my car. God has been talking to me about my life living up to, and being an example of, *Echad*. *Echad* for me is not for the observer but for the displayer, it is the talking "to me" part that matters. It

---

[15] 4 Hear, O Israel: The LORD our God, the LORD is One (*Echad*). (Deu 6:4 NIV)

is for me. A reminder of who I am and who loves me. I have a license plate that says *Echad.* The local Rabbi tells his congregation to look at my license plate as they pass my pharmacy. He understands the word *Echad.* The more I wear it on my hat and shirt and the more I drive around with it on my car license plate, the more I realize that I am not alone, that my actions which emanate from my inward self must match this word because I have constant company. The relationship with the Holy Spirit drives me to be consistent with the meaning of this word. It does not matter whether it's the local Jewish congregation who knows about my license plate or my family, or individuals who come to my service or those who read my book. I realize that I must live with focus because I represent the God who uses this word to describe Himself. It is for me.

The Standard

God has offered us, humans, a standard, Jesus the Messiah. Jesus has sent the Holy Spirit. Human good works, because of human brokenness, cannot be the standard. We all know this. Therefore, it is easy or easier for humans to not have any standard of living from a godly perspective. Many people claim their faith is personal and inward and that is exactly what the demonic wants. Clouded faith. People want the organization to be their witness. This is not the biblical example. The biblical example is that the faith relationship is experienced inside and wants to explode into manifestations. When Israel traveled in the desert for 40 years the relationship with this God was for them, it was visible. This is God's message to those of us who came after because is it visible to us[16]. If an Israelite went to a nearby town and decided to partake of the local barbecue festival, the message for those other people was not that the Israelite was breaking laws but that he was breaking relationship with his God, a visible God at that! Something inside of him was broken. He had no standard. This is what Adam and Eve realized also, something inside of them had changed. Back then, as it is today, relationship with God appeared to mean following rules and performing habits. But that was only the appearance. It was not the Standard. It was about

---

[16] *that is* the Spirit of truth, whom the world cannot receive, because it does not see Him or know Him, but you know Him because He lives with you, and will be in you. (Joh 14:17 NAS)

the same event then as it is today, a rapport, a connection, a bond. Relationship with God is not about a set of rules attached to cultural expressions or habits. True relationship with God is that which occurs on the inside enough to make change on the outside.

I believe that it is imperative for Kingdom citizens to make sure they know who they are and hold themselves accountable to and how they should be living their lives. Not their haircut, or their clothing, or their holidays, but an inward relationship that drives their actions, mannerisms, ethics, and morals. There is the thread that is Israel. It exists over the millennia and the Messiah Jesus is pulling on it. When He pulls that thread, will you move, are you attached to it? If you think your church, your organization, your denomination, or religion has anything to do with being a Kingdom Citizen, beware! Kingdom Citizenship happens when, like Jesus, you HEAR the Holy Spirit directly and walk with the Holy Spirit, and one does not ignore His voice, because The Holy Spirit is the thread. This is the Standard.

On Your House and On Your Gates

I wear *Echad* on my hat because it testifies inside and out that I am attached to the thread. I recite the Hebrew prayer called Shema because I am attached to the thread. Part of the words of this prayer call the reciter to write the words of God on their house and on their gates, to wear it on their foreheads and on their hands. This doesn't mean to get a tattoo (but you can if it is meaningful, the right meaningful); relationship simply means the active and ongoing connection with the Holy Spirit keeps you attached to the thread. Kingdom citizens are attached to the thread. They are individuals who follow the God of Israel, The Father, Jesus the Messiah and the Holy Spirit. This is the mystery.

Notes.

---

[i] Years ago, I had a dream. Not your typical dream. It was a dream from the Holy Spirit. I was reminded of it when writing this book because of its significance concerning my walk with God. I want to share it with you. I was in a house, a house of worship and I wanted to get out, but I could not. I was so desperate that I was going to jump out the window and the window moved to a height I could not reach. As I was panicking, an elevator door opened and there was a man standing there. He beckoned me in, and the elevator went down one level. When I exited, I realized I was in the foundation of the building but, it was more than that. There was much work going on. It was almost like a convention. Many workers were present. Then at one point I grabbed one of the walls and it moved wherever I pushed it. I was in awe! God always has Kingdom Citizens working in the foundations of His Kingdom. And we can move walls and supports and any part of the structure we need to in order to make it work for His Kingdom. But you must be in the foundation. The upper level is just an organizational prison. Jesus sets us free!

John's other Books

www.ingramcontent.com/pod-product-compliance
Lightning Source LLC
Chambersburg PA
CBHW051338150726
47997CB00004B/1522